The Wonderful World of Peanuts

Selected Cartoons from MORE PEANUTS.
Vol. 1

Charles M. Schulz

CORONET BOOKS
Hodder Fawcett, London

Copyright © 1952, 1953, 1954 by
United Feature Syndicate, Inc.

First published by
Fawcett Publications Inc., New York

Coronet edition 1971
Seventh impression 1977

Printed in Great Britain for
Hodder Fawcett Ltd.,
Mill Road, Dunton Green, Sevenoaks, Kent
by C. Nicholls & Company Ltd
The Philips Park Press, Manchester

ISBN 0 340 12543 8

ARE YOU GOING TO NURSERY SCHOOL THESE DAYS, LUCY?

YES, I'VE BEEN REINSTATED

IS IT FUN?

IS IT FUN?! ALL WE HAVE TO DO EVERY DAY IS PLAY PLAY PLAY PLAY PLAY PLAY...

I'VE NEVER BEEN SO BORED IN ALL MY LIFE!

SCHULZ

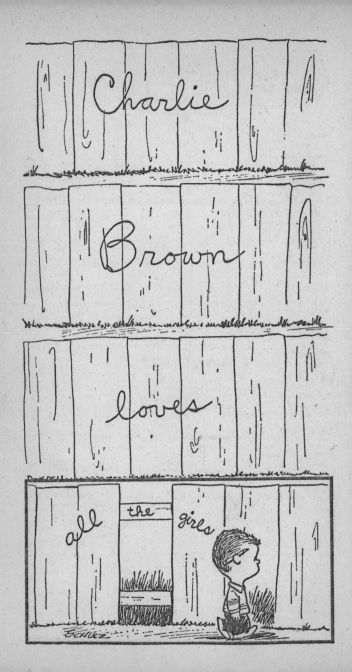

SCHULZ

SHERMY!
TRY IT AGAIN..
SHERMY
I'LL BE RIGHT OUT..
THANKS, LUCY...IF I NEED YOU AGAIN, I'LL LET YOU KNOW..
SCHULZ

And don't forget about all the other PEANUTS books in Coronet Book editions. Good Grief! More than 3 million of them in paperback! See the check-list overleaf.

© 1970 United Feature Syndicate, Inc.

Wherever Paperbacks Are Sold

FOR THE LOVE OF PEANUTS

All these books are available at your local bookshop or newsagent, or can be ordered direct from the publisher. Just tick the titles you want and fill in the form below.
Prices and availability subject to change without notice.

CORONET BOOKS, P.O. Box 11, Falmouth, Cornwall.
Please send cheque or postal order, and allow the following for postage and packing:
U.K. – One book 19p plus 9p per copy for each additional book ordered, up to a maximum of 73p.
B.F.P.O. and EIRE – 19p for the first book plus 9p per copy for the next 6 books, thereafter 3p per book.
OTHER OVERSEAS CUSTOMERS – 20p for the first book and 10p per copy for each additional book.

Name ....

Address ....

....